Yellow Umbrella Books are published by Red Brick Learning
7825 Telegraph Road, Bloomington, Minnesota 55438
http://www.redbricklearning.com

Library of Congress Cataloging-in-Publication Data
    Shepard, Daniel 1957–
    Numbers all around/by Daniel Shepard.
    p. cm.
    Summary: "Simple text and photos introduce the concept that numbers are
everywhere"—Provided by publisher.
    Includes index.
    ISBN-13: 978-0-7368-5982-0 (hardcover)
    ISBN-10: 0-7368-5982-9 (hardcover)
    ISBN 0-7368-1695-X
    1. Number concept—Juvenile literature. I. Title.
QA141.3.S54 2006
513—dc22   2005025746

Written by Daniel Shepard
Developed by Raindrop Publishing

Editorial Director: Mary Lindeen
Editor: Jennifer VanVoorst
Photo Researcher: Wanda Winch
Conversion Assistants: Jenny Marks, Laura Manthe

Photo Credits
Cover: PhotoLink/PhotoDisc; Title Page: Grantpix/Index Stock; Page 4: Gary
Sundermeyer/Capstone Press; Page 6: AFP/Corbis; Page 8: Carl and Ann Purcell/Corbis;
Page 10: S. Meltzer/PhotoLink/PhotoDisc; Page 12: Gary Sundermeyer/Capstone Press;
Page 14: Steve Allen/Brand X Pictures; Page 16: DigitalVision

1 2 3 4 5 6 11 10 09 08 07 06

Numbers All Around

by Daniel Shepard

Yellow Umbrella Books
for early readers

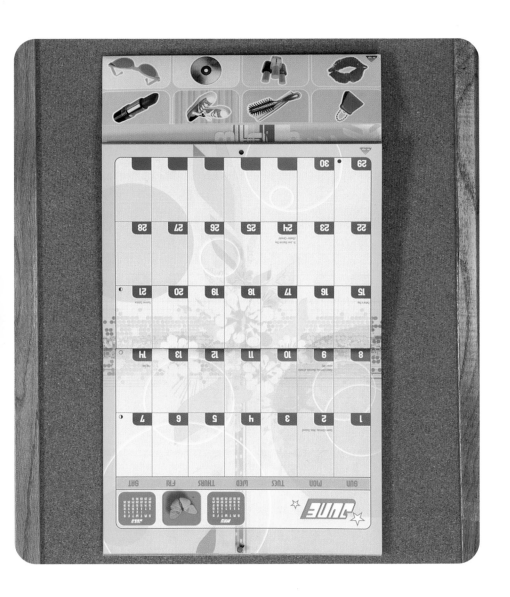

I see numbers on the wall.

I see numbers on
the clock.

I see numbers in the store.

I see numbers on the team.

I see numbers on
the house.

I see numbers on
the truck.

Numbers are all around!

Index